Fireworks

Snakes, Eyeballs and Indians

SKILLS BOOK

gill & macmillan primary

Gill & Macmillan
Hume Avenue
Park West
Dublin 12
www.gillmacmillan.ie

ISBN: 9780717153152

Design: Outburst Design / Aisli Madden
Cover illustration: Aisli Madden
Inside illustrations: Derry Dillon
Printed and bound in Italy by L.E.G.O. SpA

First published June 2012

Acknowledgements
Extract from *Thunder and Lightnings* © Jan Mark, 1976. Reprinted by permission of David Higham Associates, Ltd. Extract from *The Exiles* © Hilary McKay, 1991. Reprinted by permission of Hodder Children's Books, a division of Hachette Children's Books.

Photo credit pg 39: *Getty Images.*

The authors and publisher have made every effort to trace all copyright holders, but if any has been inadvertently overlooked we would be pleased to make the necessary arrangement at the first opportunity.

Contents

The London Eye Mystery

Word bank

unique sightseeing arced anti-clockwise gene pool mosher casual cool overhead dishrag devastation icon consignment trolley tracking schedule souvenir backdrop precisely convenience burly commuter slithered oesophagus re-materialize remotely livid

A. Wish you were here

Salim and Auntie Glo were sightseeing in London on their way to a new life in New York. Have you ever been sightseeing? Send a postcard to a friend from one of your sightseeing trips.

B. A challenging life

1. *Ted's brain has its 'own unique operating system' which colours the way he interprets the world and how he reacts to every day events.* What do you think is meant by this sentence in the introduction?

2. Does what you have read in the text support the fact that Ted is different in some way? Give examples.

____

____

____

____

3. Write your thoughts on how this makes life challenging for him.

____

____

____

____

____

____

C. Using the dictionary

1. To understand what we read we need to know the meaning of the words in the text. Find the meanings of the following words by

- rereading the text
- guessing the meaning
- looking them up the dictionary.

Word	I think it means	Dictionary meaning
1. unique		
2. impressed		
3. devastation		
4. icon		
5. consignment		
6. convenience		
7. commuter		
8. oesophagus		

2. Some long words are easier to pronounce and spell when you divide them up into smaller units (syllables). Use the words from question 1 and divide them into syllables.

Word	Syllable 1	Syllable 2	Syllable 3	Syllable 4
unique				
impressed				
devastation				
icon				
consignment				
commuter				
convenience				
oesophagus				

3. Sometimes we use phrases or idioms which are not meant to be taken literally. For example, Salim tells Ted that the play *The Tempest* would be right up his street. What does the author mean by that?

____

____

4. Rewrite the following idioms taken from the story in your own words. What do you notice about your answers?

- drives him bananas ______________________
- drive you nuts ______________________
- drive her round the bend ______________________
- off your trolley ______________________

5. Now explain what these idioms mean:

1. She wouldn't say *boo to a goose.* ______________________

   ____
2. That boy is *wet behind the ears*! ______________________

   ____
3. He *got out on the wrong side of the bed.* ______________________

   ____
4. Mum has *a bee in her bonnet* about table manners. ______________________

   ____

D. The grammar highway

1. Match the words below with their meanings.

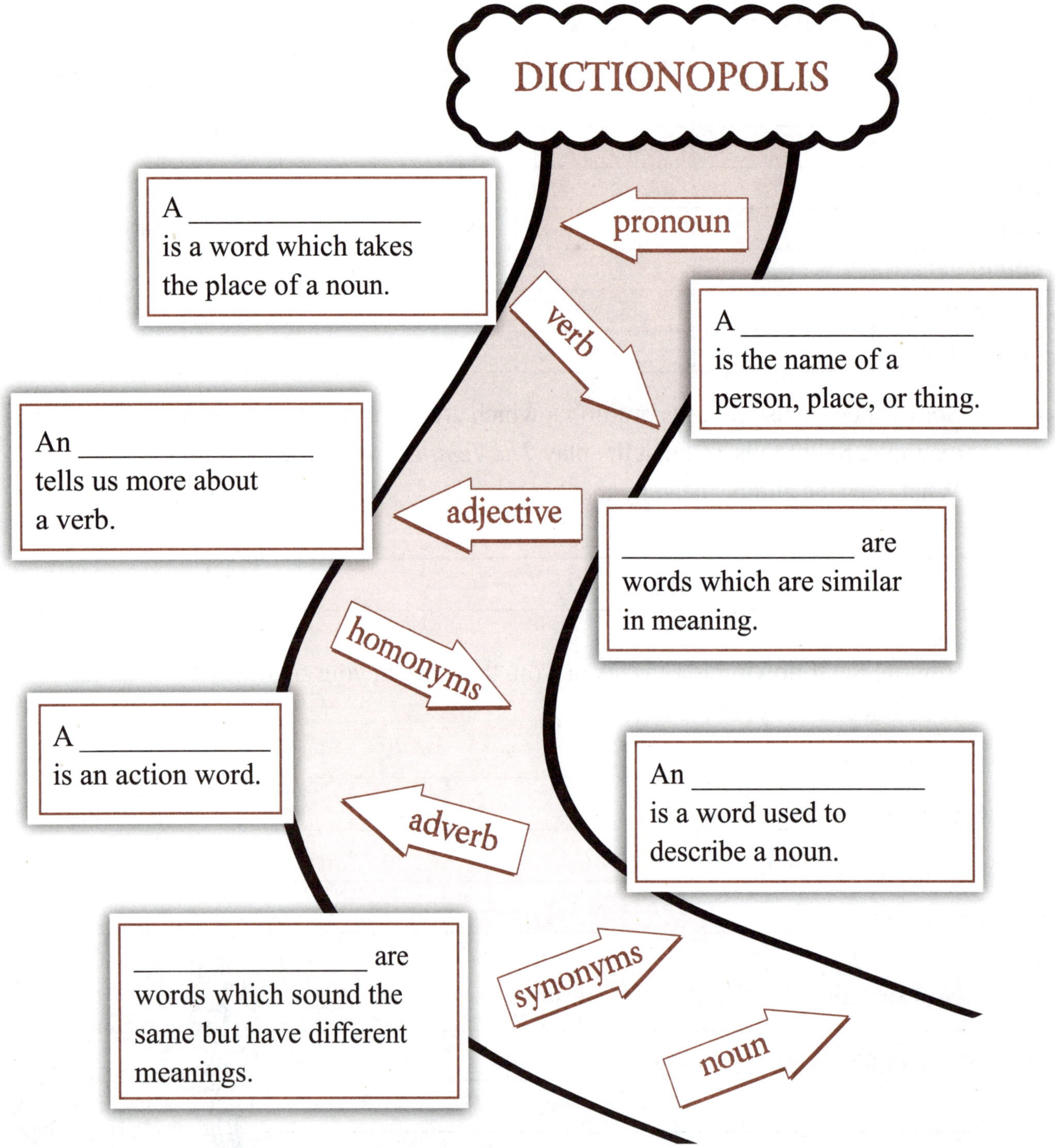

2. Scan the text *The London Eye Mystery* and find two examples of each of the above.

Pronouns	Verbs	Adjectives	Homonyms	Adverbs	Synonyms	Nouns

E. Be a director

1. When Salim's pod landed and the doors opened, many different characters emerged. Use your text to list the characters.

wed am Ryan
Thurs pm
Fri am

2. What do you think people talked about in the pod? Choose any two characters and write the conversation that took place between them.
Remember that a script of a conversation is not written as a narrative or a story. Each time a new character speaks you must start on a new line. Scripts tell us how the characters speak but can also give directions as to how or whether they move.

3. Picture the characters using information the author gives in the text, your own imagination and your knowledge of characters in books and people in real life. Illustrate the characters to show what they might have looked like.

Character 1 Name:	Character 2 Name:	Character 3 Name:

F. Tired words

1. Kat calls lots of things cute! She *overuses* the word. This is one of those 'tired words' we use too often. Replace the word cute in the following sentences. Use a thesaurus to help you.

1. I have a very cute friend. ______________________

   ____

2. Baby kittens are always very cute. ______________________

   ____

3. David Beckham is a cute football player. ______________________

   ____

4. There's a very cute movie star in that film. ______________________

   ____

5. That model is modelling a very cute skirt. ______________________

   ____

6. Our baby brother is very cute. ______________________

   ____

2. Replace the tired word said in these sentences.

1. 'The lion escaped from the zoo,' she said. ______________________________

2. My baby brother said 'don't tell on me!' ______________________________

3. 'The flight to Rome is about to leave,' the air hostess said. ______________________________

4. 'Give me back my good pen,' my sister said. ______________________________

5. She said that poem very well. ______________________________

6. 'Will you mend the puncture on my bike?' she said. ______________________________

All the fun of the fair

Correct the mistakes in the sentences and rewrite the whole sentence.

1. The word 'fair' comes from the Greek word for holiday. ______________________________

2. Dodgem cars were invented in 1827. ______________________________

3. The first helter-skelter appeared at a funfair in Manchester in 1906. ______________________________

4. The London Eye is located on the banks of the River Liffey. ______________________________

5. Malt Disney opened Disneyland in 1955. ______________________________

6. The fastest roller-coaster is located in Japan. ____________________

____

7. Candyfloss machines were invented in Canada in the 1920s. ____________________

____

8. England's best known funfair is *Funderland*. ____________________

____

9. It is possible to see a distance of 20 miles from the London Eye. ____________________

____

10. The Ferris wheel was invented to rival the Colosseum in Rome. ____________________

____

Clever challenges

1. What is meant by the phrase cultural icon? Choose one person you think is a modern cultural icon. Write a paragraph about this person explaining why you think he, or she, deserves the title.

2. What cultural icon would you most like to meet and why?

3. Write an acrostic poem about an individual who you think is a 'mosher'.

____________________ is a mosher coz

M ____________________

O ____________________

S ____________________

H ____________________

E ____________________

R ____________________

4. Use the information in *All the fun of the fair* to summarise the key points in the history of fairs. Give the names of different fairs, the year in which they first started, their place of origin and details about them.

Anneli the Art Hater

Word bank

dabbed loathed smudging pastel collage non-toxic interminable chaotic encouraging warped grubbier endeavours averted gamble sporadically straggled sagged register surreptitious wheedled ivory ermine molten droning gritty spangled scooped reputation feigning discarded irritated laboriously banisters threaded overstuffed joss-stick embroidery patchwork enamelled bespattered exceedingly proclaimed panelling vaguely pottered

A. Art terms

There are some art terms used by the author in this story. Here is a list of them with a number of others added. Write out what each one means.

pastel		model	
collage		charcoal	
brush work		tempera	
construction		mono print	
bayer		impressionism	
aquarelle		pointillism	
canvas		gallery	
embroidery		exhibition	

B. Antiques in the attic

Make a list of things that might be stored in an attic. You can use your knowledge of your own attic at home or attics you have read about in books.

C. Colour mix

In the story Miss Pears is 'mixing more pink'. What colours is she mixing to get pink? Do you know how to mix colours? In your copybook, make a colour mixing chart like the one below.

Example

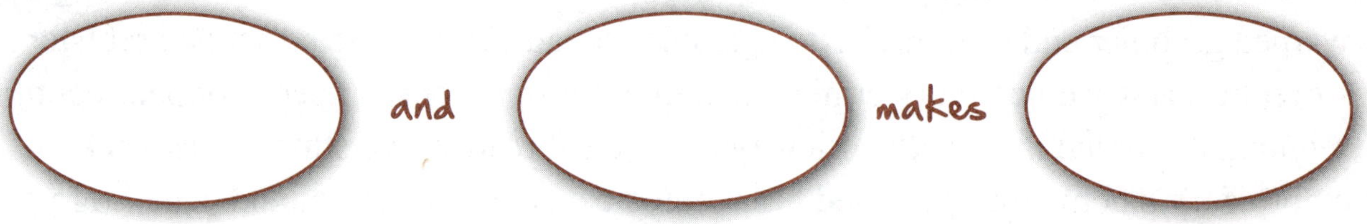

D. Powerful verbs

Our writing could be much more interesting if we use verbs that liven up what we are trying to say.

Example

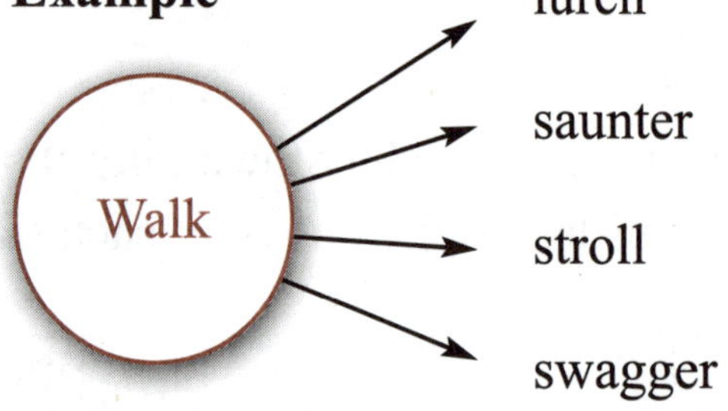

1. Find livelier verbs similar in meaning to the verbs below which would improve your writing. Use a thesaurus to help you.

eat __________ __________ __________ __________	run __________ __________ __________ __________	say __________ __________ __________ __________
jump __________ __________ __________ __________	look __________ __________ __________ __________	get __________ __________ __________ __________
talk __________ __________ __________ __________	like __________ __________ __________ __________	close __________ __________ __________ __________

2. Select four of your new verbs and use each one in a sentence.

____

____

____

____

E. Be a reporter

Definition box

A report for a newspaper or magazine is written in a different style to a story or a letter. A reporter asks many questions before beginning to write.

1. Pretend that Anneli finds an amazing treasure in the attic. Imagine that you are a reporter in the local newspaper and you are sent to interview her. What questions will you ask her? What answers do you imagine she will give you?

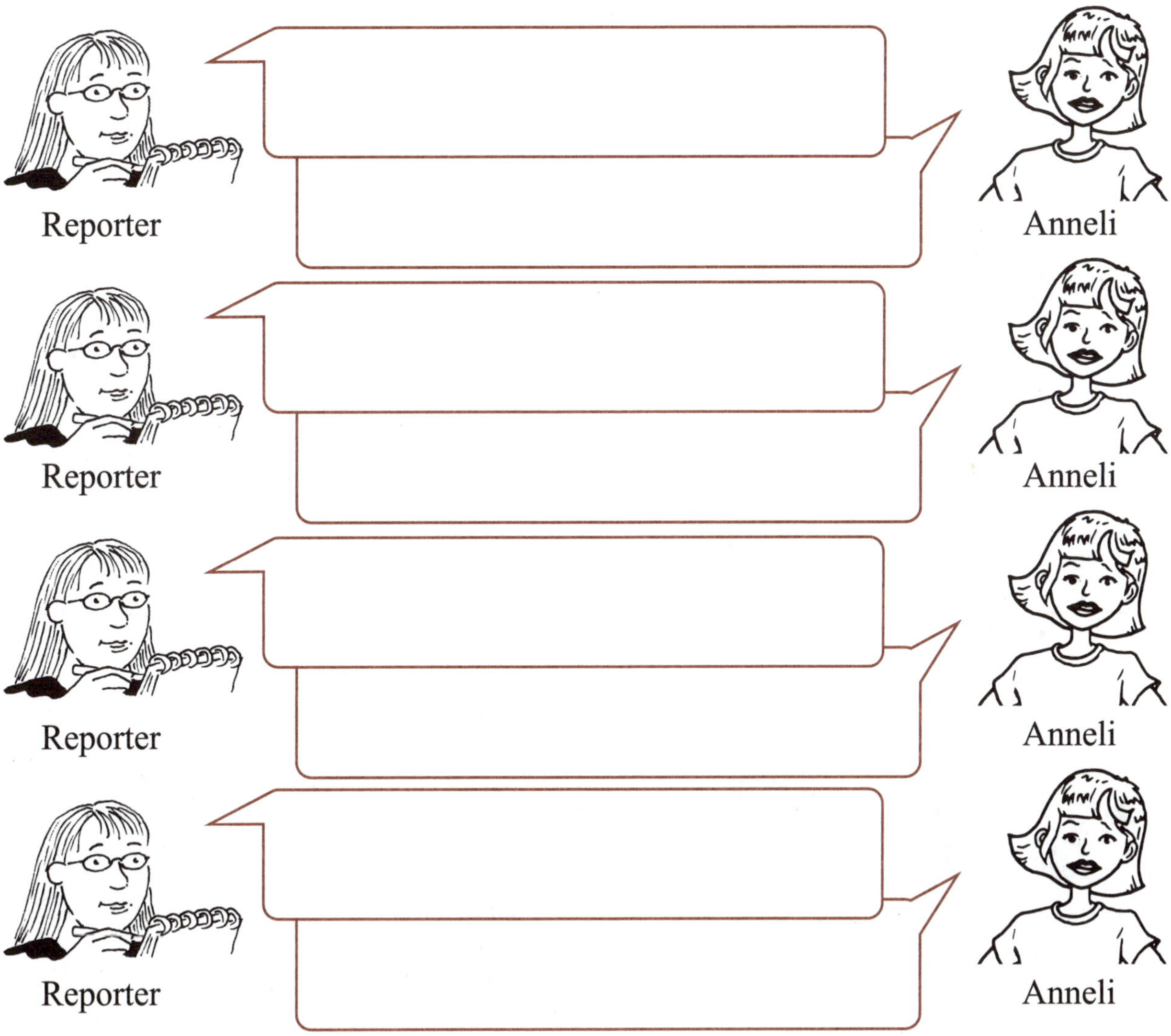

2. In your copybook, write the report for the editor of the newspaper using the headline below.

Amazing Treasure Find

F. Vocabulary hunt

1. In this excerpt the author, Anne Fine, uses a rich and interesting vocabulary. The extra information this provides helps us to visualise the story all the more clearly. Carry out a word hunt for the following parts of speech by revisiting the story. List your words in the table below.

Verbs	Adverbs	Nouns	Adjectives	Prepositions	Pronouns

2. There is a vivid description of the character of Miss Pears in the story. Read *Anneli the Art Hater* again, and describe Miss Pears using the author's and your own words.

3. Think of another book where the author describes a character using exceptionally descriptive language. Write your description of that character.

The National Gallery of Ireland

1. Look at the information leaflet on The National Gallery of Ireland in your Anthology. Use this to complete the table below giving the same key information but presenting it in a shorter form.

Location	Opening hours	Tours/lectures	Food	Shopping

2. Which of the two ways of presenting the information did you find easier to follow and why?

____

____

____

3. Write five key facts about The National Gallery of Ireland based on the leaflet you have read.

____

____

____

____

____

Clever challenges

1. Complete *one* of the following paragraph starters:

   - *My favourite character in this story is* _______________ *because...*
   - *The character I liked least in this story was* _________________ *because...*

2. There are *two* distinct parts to the excerpt from *Anneli the Art Hater*. The first deals with the art class, while the second deals with Anneli's home life, and her discovery of the attic. How do you think these two sections might be connected? Predict how the two ideas might be linked later in the story.

3. Do you think that Anneli dislikes art for the simple reason that it is too messy, or are her reasons more complex? For example, does she believe her own ideas are not good enough?
   Write what you think her reasons are. Use evidence from the text to support your view.

4. Which item would you like to find in a secret hidden attic?

   - A painting by a famous artist
   - A bag of ancient coins
   - A box of antique toys
   - A chest of clothes that are a hundred years old
   - An alien spacecraft
   - A book of magical spells.

   Imagine that you really *did* find one of these items. Describe how you discovered it and what happened next. Imagine what the discovery looked like and draw a vivid picture of it.

5. Write a short paragraph describing Vermeer's *Lady Writing a Letter, with her Maid*, to be used by the tour guide in The National Gallery of Ireland.

The Indian in the Cupboard

Word bank

unimpressed petrified undoubtedly cautiously crouching bronze headband huddled rigid defiant coherent pigtail ballooned leggings gigantic fantastically moccasins grimace reasonable ferociously absurd brave baffled thundering jolted minuscule torso buckskin thong intricate beadwork encrusted

A. Surprise presents

1. Which of your toys would you like to come to life? Imagine that you had put this toy in the cupboard and woke up next morning to find it alive, just like Omri. Write the opening paragraph of your story. Begin as follows:

In the morning there was no doubt about it. The noise actually woke me...

2. Omri is 'unimpressed' with the plastic toy Indian he is given for his birthday! Have you ever been unimpressed by a present you were given? Write about such a time and include the following information:

- Who gave you the present?
- What was the occasion?
- Were you expecting something else?
- What were your feelings when you saw what the present was?
- Do you believe in the saying 'It's the thought that counts'? Why?

3. Omri was petrified when he heard the noise from inside the cupboard. The word petrified is better than the overused word scared. Think of other words that could be used instead of scared. Use your dictionary and thesaurus.

B. Prepositions

Definition box

A preposition is a word used before a noun or pronoun to show place, time and position.

Example
The book is on the table.
She arrived in time for school.

1. Compose sentences using the prepositions below.

1. at ____________________
2. around ____________________
3. down ____________________
4. beside ____________________
5. beneath ____________________
6. for ____________________
7. of ____________________
8. below ____________________
9. through ____________________
10. by ____________________

2. Choose from the prepositions above to complete these sentences.

1. The buzzing bees circled ____________ the heavily scented flowers.
2. A small head appeared sheepishly from ____________ the oak table.
3. The hungry child peered ____________ the cake shop window.
4. The explorers stared in amazement ____________ the strange sight before their eyes.
5. The exhausted group trudged ____________ the winding road that led to the cottage.
6. The funny novel ____________ the well-known author is a favourite ____________ our class.
7. When the bright, shiny car drew up ____________ the pathway, we all stared.
8. There was a carpet ____________ bluebells ____________ the trees.

3. Use each of these prepositions and their opposites in the same sentence.

on	above	off	up	to
inside	from	below	down	outside

Example
He walked over the hill and under the bridge.

____

____

____

____

____

____

C. Word work – syllables

Breaking words into syllables or small sound units makes them easier to pronounce, read and spell.

Example
for/got/ten

1. Look at the following words from this story and break them up into syllables.

Word	Syllables	Number of syllables
unimpressed		
perfectly		
extraordinary		
scrabbling		
immediately		
darting		
marvellous		
miniature		
reasonable		
ferociously		
absurd		

2. Compile lists of one, two, three and four syllable words. Use your Anthology to help you.

One syllable words	Two syllable words	Three syllable words	Four syllable words
cake	re/fuse	tel/e/phone	gen/er/a/tion

3. Break up the following words into syllables and write them into your copybook.

amusement	photography	facility	confession	biology	interference	cigarette
predicament	compartment	shocking	hamburger	misunderstood	guardian	

4. Make as many smaller words as you can from this long word.

Disadvantageous

D. Presenting characters

The author, Lynne Reid Banks, has created two very interesting characters for us in this story. We learn more about Omri and the Indian, Little Bull, from the descriptive language she uses to tell us about them.

1. Reread the excerpt and find *words* or *phrases* which help us get to know Omri and his Indian friend.

Omri	The Indian

2. Compare and contrast the two characters from your own point of view.

I think Omri is ______________________________ because ______________

____

____.

I think Little Bull is ____________________________ because ______________

____

____.

3. Which character would you like to meet and why? Imagine you had to introduce him to your class. Write the speech you would give.

____

____

____

____

____

____

____

____

____

____

____

Native Americans

1. Answer the following questions using complete sentences.

1. How did Native Americans come to be called Indians? ________

____

2. Why did the arrival of Europeans lead to the deaths of so many Native Americans? ________

____

3. Describe what a *powwow* is. ________

____

4. From what part of the world do archaeologists agree Native Americans originally came from? ________

____

5. Do all Native Americans have the same customs and lifestyles? Why (not)?

____

____

6. Do you think that Native Americans have been fairly portrayed in films? Why?

____

____

7. Write a definition for each of the following terms.

- totem ________
- squash ________
- wickiup ________
- appaloosa ________
- adobe ________
- reservation ________

2. Complete the following.

I learned that Native Americans ____________________

I also learned that ____________________

I had never known that ____________________

I was surprised to learn that ____________________

I found it really interesting that ____________________

Clever challenges

1. Draw a portrait of the Indian based on the descriptions in the excerpt from *The Indian in the Cupboard.*

2. Omri is planning to keep the Indian a secret from his parents and his brothers. Have you ever kept a secret from your parents? Do you think this is a good idea? Make a case for and against keeping secrets.

3. Have a class debate on keeping secrets using the ideas in the exercise above.

4. Research the history of one of the following:

   - Sitting Bull
   - Pocahontas
   - Geronimo
   - The Battle of the Little Bighorn
   - Wounded Knee

   Present your findings to your class.

5. What did the Indian on the beach in the poem 'There was an Indian' see for the first time in his life when the Europeans landed? Imagine the scene. Make a list of what you think he saw.

   Example
   white skin

Olivia Kidney: Hot on the Trail

Word bank

gleefully chirpy aerobics pasty piñata pregnant deflated handyman brownstone zoned suppress requisite smirk chronic murky thwacked whippet leotard alcove freak baloney humiliation assigned incredulously squirming indecent demurred hedged

A. Morning vs night

'Olivia Kidney had never been much of a morning person.' Do you think you would be described as a morning person or a night person? Write a brief description of each personality type.

Morning person	Night person

B. Persuasion

Olivia is about to go to a special school for gifted and talented children. Do you think this a good or bad idea? Write five arguments *for* and five *against* schools for talented children in your copybook.

C. My rucksack

Read again the description of everything that was in Olivia's rucksack/schoolbag. Now write a description of what is in your own rucksack using lots of descriptive words.

D. Adjectives

Definition box

Authors use adjectives to tell us more about (or to describe) nouns. There are different sorts of adjectives. Some tell us about quantity, quality and possession. Others are called interrogative adjectives (*asking* which or what thing is meant) and demonstrative adjectives (*showing* which or what thing is meant).

1. Look at the list of different types of adjectives below and compose sentences to show you understand how to use them. Write your sentences in your copybook.

Quantity	Quality	Possession	Interrogative	Demonstrative
much	wise	his/her	which	this
little	old	your	whose	that
any	good	our	what	these
some	fresh	their		those

2. Read the story and list all the adjectives you find and say which category above they belong to.

Adjective	Category	Adjective	Category

3. Find adjectives in the story which are used to describe these.

Olivia	Bus people	Subway people	The school

4. From what you have learned so far explain how adjectives improve a piece of writing.

____

____

____

E. Sentences – simple and multiple

Definition box

There are different kinds of sentences.

Example

'Mary had a little lamb' is a simple sentence. It cannot be broken into smaller sentences or clauses.

'Mary had a little lamb and its fleece was white as snow' is a multiple sentence because it is made up of two clauses or sentences joined by the link word (or conjunction) and. Each clause can stand on its own:
Mary had a little lamb.
Its fleece was white as snow.

1. Use and, or, or but to join these sentences.

1. I told my mother. She ignored me. _______________

____

2. I travelled by car. Mum went by taxi. _______________

____

3. I must find my schoolbag quickly. I will be late for school. _______________

____

4. I wanted a bicycle. I hadn't saved enough money. _______________

____

5. He called to my house. I gave him some lemonade. _______________

____

6. Keep away from the edge of the stream. You might fall in. _______________

____

2. Compose six sentences using the link words/conjunctions.

Clever challenges

1. Olivia's dad *talked in food terms a lot*, for example

   You have what they call raw talent. All it needs is a little seasoning.

   Olivia herself feels that she could never get into the school even if she were covered in barbeque sauce. Other 'food' phrases include sweet as pie/cheesed off. Write five new 'food' sentences.

2. Olivia obviously has had to change schools a number of times. Have you ever had to change school? List the worries you would have if you were told you had to move school tomorrow.

3. 'I don't believe in ghosts,' Olivia states. Do you agree with her? Complete one of the following paragraph starters.

   - *I believe in ghosts because...*
   - *I do not believe in ghosts because...*
   - *I am not sure whether or not I believe in ghosts. This is because...*

4. Use the Internet to find a map of one of the following:
   - The New York Subway System
   - The London Underground
   - The Paris Metro.

   Print out one map and explore some of the stations marked on it e.g. the Louvre in Paris or the Yankee Stadium in New York. Choose one and research it.

5. Olivia had a talent for belching the letters of the alphabet! Make up eight really funny or silly talents that might get you accepted into a 'special' school like Olivia's.

Wilderness

Word bank

husky safari sled veranda tree-lined crash helmet charging panicky hitch snowmobile reindeer nudged rogue unhitching swaying numb compass disloyal boomed concentrate charged

A. Expressing an opinion

Do you think that Tom and Johnny are being brave or reckless in setting out to find their Mum? Using evidence from your text to support your opinion, complete both of these paragraph starters in your copybook.

- *I think they are being brave. This is because...*
- *I think they are being reckless. This is because...*

Give both your paragraphs to a partner to judge which argument is stronger.

B. Comfort food

1. What does the phrase 'comfort food' mean? Write your own definition of it.

____

____

2. Hot chocolate features in this story as comfort food. Make a list of your comfort foods, foods that make you feel better when you are fed up.

C. Similes

Definition box

A simile is a figure of speech in which one thing or person is compared to another using *as* or *like*. These often become well-known phrases, e.g. *He is as snug as a bug in a rug.*

1. Complete these well-known similes.

as cool as a ____________	as blind as a ____________
as daft as a ____________	as gentle as a ____________
as black as ____________	as strong as an ____________
My love is like a red, ________	sleep like a ____________
float like a ____________	sting like a ____________
He is like a ________ with a sore head.	to eat like a ____________

2. Now compose your own endings using some of the above starters.

____

____

____

____

____

____

____

____

____

____

D. Writing an epilogue

Definition box

An epilogue is a short summary of the events that happen *after* the main story has ended.

This extract ends with *They charged through the dark. They went under high, thick trees. They felt them, right over their heads, and it was even darker. Tom could see nothing. He could hear the dogs, but he couldn't see them.*

1. You have been asked to write the epilogue for the story *Wilderness*, how do you think it will go? Brainstorm your ideas first. Write down key words and phrases which you can use.

__________ __________ ____________________

__________ __________ ____________________

__________ __________ ____________________

__________ __________ ____________________

2. Now, taking your ideas, words and key phrases into account, begin the process of writing the epilogue as an author does.

Your first draft

____

____

____

____

____

____

____

____

____

3. Proofread your work.

4. Edit your ideas, grammar, spelling and punctuation, and then redraft.

5. Write a final draft of your work and share what you have written with a partner, a group or the class.

Final draft

E. Research writing

Tom and Johnny are on a husky safari holiday in Finland with their mother.
What do you already know about Finland?
What does the text of this story tell you about Finland?
Where can you find out more information about Finland?
Record your information in the KWL chart.

K What I already know about Finland	W What I want to know about Finland	L What I have learned about Finland

My research tools: ______________________________

What I learned about doing research:

____

____

____

____

Antarctic explorers

Comprehension questions

Answer the following questions about polar exploration using properly constructed, full sentences.

1. Name some of the dangers involved in polar exploration. ______________________________

____

____

2. How far is it from the coast of Antarctica to the South Pole? ______________________________

____

3. Name the two explorers who tried to reach the South Pole in 1910. ______________________________

____

4. What were the final words spoken by Captain Oates? ____________________

____

5. What single advantage helped Amundsen reach the Pole first? ____________

____

6. What enormous challenge did Shackleton set himself? ________________

____

7. Name one way in which Tom Crean demonstrated his bravery. ___________

____

8. Do you think reaching the South Pole today would be easier than in 1910? Why? ____

____

9. What is a glacier? ____

____

10. Would the South Pole explorers have had to be wary of polar bears? Why?

____

Me and My Brother

Do your parents have particular sayings that they use over and over again? Draw a funny cartoon of them and put their sayings into speech bubbles. Give it to them as a surprise present.

Clever challenges

The boys in the story *Wilderness* are on an adventure holiday. Would you like to go on an adventure holiday? Choose one holiday from the list below, imagine what it would involve and write about it.

- A mountain climbing holiday
- A skiing holiday
- A jungle trekking holiday
- A river rafting holiday
- A yachting holiday
- A caravanning/camper van holiday
- A diving holiday

Framed

Word bank

oasis marvel framed recovery low loader recovery antifreeze Hyundai Daihatsu marshmallow tweezers admired Monopoly obviously physics situation workshop mix-up log supply demand bargain disrespect forecourt offside baldy database sourced unbeatable acquisitions tailgate intercooler barracuda balaclava customized nasal ninja obsessed super-poseable articulation walloped keeled seduced criminality photocopier

A. Know your cars

1. How many different types of car can you name? Write them into the grid below.

Nissan Juke			
			Ford Focus

2. If you could have your own car what make and model would you choose? Complete this paragraph starter.

I would like to drive a ______________________. This is because ____________

____

3. You tell can tell what county a car is originally from by reading its registration number. Research the registration codes from all the counties and complete the following table (work in alphabetical order).

C	Cork				
				WW	Wicklow

4. Write a new entry for Dylan's petrol log below.

Name of car owner: ____________________

Make and model of vehicle: ____________________

Registration number: ____________________

Observations: ____________________

____

____

Comments: ____________________

____

Write some other entries in your copybook.

5. Correct the following statements.

1. Mrs Stannard owned a red Ford Mondeo. ____________________
2. Oil is the same as antifreeze. ____________________
3. The top speed of a Daihatsu Copen is 206 mph. ____________________
4. Dylan's family took a trip to the seaside at Ballybunion. ____________________
5. Dylan's family played Twister in the caravan. ____________________
6. Dylan's Mum bought the petrol log at an antique fair. ____________________
7. Mr Morgan's car had two bald front tyres. ____________________
8. Daft Tom owned a green mountain bike. ____________________
9. Daft Tom wore a Superman cycling helmet. ____________________
10. Mum bought the printer at the charity shop for £40. ____________________

B. Prefixes

Definition box

A prefix is a group of letters put before a word which changes its meaning.

List words that follow these prefixes and think of one more prefix for the last box.

sub- (under) submarine	tele- (far/distant) telephone	be- (off/away) behead
dis- (not/apart) discover	ex- (out) express	re- (back/again) return
super- (above) supernatural	trans- (across) transatlantic	

2. Choose a word from the box below to complete each of the following sentences.

repair	telescope	supervisor	transfer
subterranean	absorb	beheaded	exports

1. Many cities have ______________ trains which run underground.
2. The plumber came to __________ the burst pipe.
3. I ironed a __________ onto my jeans.
4. Galileo was an astronomer who used a ___________.
5. Ireland __________ dairy products to other countries.
6. Plants ___________ water from the ground.
7. A ____________ is often in charge of an office.
8. Mary Queen of Scots was ____________.

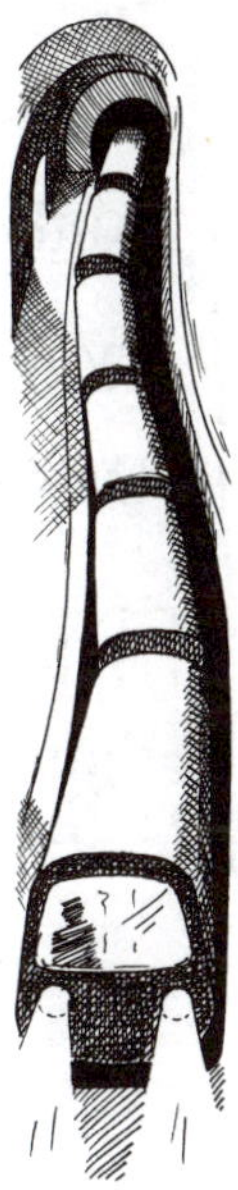

3. Use a dictionary to find ten words with prefixes and explain what the words mean.

Word	Meaning

4. Now write ten sentences in your copybook using these words. Then delete the words with prefixes and give the sentences to the person beside you to fill in.

Clever challenges

1. What did you think of the story *Wilderness*? Write a report including the following headings in your copybook.

Title:

Author:

Type of text (story/poem/drama/novel):

Date:

Before I read it I thought:	What I liked:	What I noticed:	It made me feel:

2. Look at the thermometer and mark your response to the story.

Hot warm medium lukewarm freezing

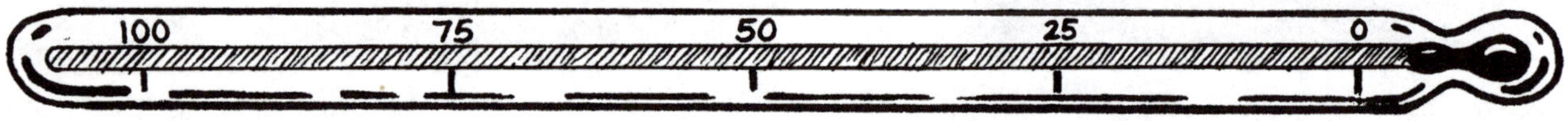

3. Repeat this exercise for other stories you have read.

A trip to the theatre

Word bank

creative programme director production rehearsals miniature lighting filters costume compiles props authentic composer specialist interval superstitious witchcraft tragedy comedy

Behind the scenes

Imagine you are a set designer for the play 'Macbeth'. Choose a witch scene from the play. Draw a picture showing the stage with the witch characters. Label your illustration and make a note of special effects you plan for the production.

The Scottish Play

A. Background

1. 

Macbeth is a play about ambition and murder. At the time when Shakespeare wrote it, people thought that witches had supernatural powers. They believed that witches could predict the future and influence people's lives by magic. Discuss your view of witches in a group and write down your group's ideas to share with the class.

2. Recreate the action of the scene in a series of cartoon pictures. Use speech bubbles to include the most interesting dialogue.

B. Writing a summary

Definition box

A summary contains only the main points of a story.

Read *The Scottish Play* and divide it into scenes. Then write a summary of each scene.

Scene 1

1. Beth and Tim arrive at the village hall on a wet and windy night.
2. ______
3. ______
4. ______
5. ______

Scene 2

1. ______
2. ______
3. ______
4. ______
5. ______

Scene 3

1. ______
2. ______
3. ______
4. ______
5. ______

Clever challenges

1. Create a character profile of a witch. Think about distinguishing features and powers. Use striking and powerful descriptions so that you influence your reader to either like or dislike your witch.

2. Imagine your class is performing *Macbeth* in school. Design a programme for producing the play and choose classmates to act the various parts or to work on the production team.

3. Imagine you attended the play in the school. The principal has asked you to write a report on the performance for the school newsletter. Include your opinions on all aspects of the production.

4. Interview one of the characters in the play for the school newsletter.

5. Look up the meaning of each word below.

   Alliteration is ____________________________________.

   Assonance is ____________________________________.

   A metaphor is ____________________________________.

6. Now find examples of them in the text.

The Demon Headmaster

Word bank

foster awkward pinched relax muttering sidled reciting waver chanting earnest accusingly smug gabbled grateful disapproving woodenly abruptly blazer unison blotch bellowed chorused utterly orderly tacked barring haughty irritated prefect deportment bewildered swivelled immaculate startlingly chatter inefficient unnervingly expression unreadable precise brain-teaser motionless botch crooned muzzily bewilderment

A. Schools and rules

1. Imagine that Dinah is arriving at a new school. This new school is your school. Write Dinah's description of your school.

____

____

____

____

2. Playgrounds need rules! What kinds of rules would ensure that a playground is a happy, safe place for everyone? Think of six sensible, worthwhile rules and design a motto and symbol for each rule in the boxes below.

3. The headmaster gave a test to Dinah to check her general knowledge and her ability. Make out a test consisting of ten items (include as many subjects as you can – Science, History, Geography, Music, Art, Maths, etc.) Give your test to a partner to do!

1. ______________________________________
2. ______________________________________
3. ______________________________________
4. ______________________________________
5. ______________________________________
6. ______________________________________
7. ______________________________________
8. ______________________________________
9. ______________________________________
10. ______________________________________

B. Adverbs

Definition box

An adverb is a word that tells us more about a verb, an adjective or another adverb.

There are many types of adverbs. They tell us about the time, place, number, degree and manner in which something was done. There are also adverbs which ask a question.

Example

1. Where did you put the box? (question)
2. That was a very good play. (degree)
3. The girl spoke once in the class. (number)
4. He will soon be here. (time)
5. She walked slowly across the meadow. (manner)

1. Circle the adverbs in the following sentences.

    1. He walked cautiously up the lane.
    2. Carefully Dinah sidled up to the first circle.
    3. His shoulders were hunched up stiffly under his thin shirt.
    4. She could hardly believe it.
    5. Dinah was suddenly annoyed.
    6. She could barely get the words out.
    7. As quietly and steadily as marching soldiers, they walked together.
    8. The questions were fairly hard.
    9. She was so nervous that she stumbled once or twice.
    10. When did he come?

2. Make adverbs out of these adjectives.

Adjective	Adverb	Adjective	Adverb
brave		attentive	
noisy		cruel	
wasteful		careless	

Now, in your copybook, put each adverb into a sentence.

3. Using interesting adverbs, write a short description in your copybook of an event in your life.

4. Underline the adverb/adverbs in each sentence below and write what *type* of adverb it is.

1. The boy was very badly hurt when he fell. ______
2. When will you arrive at your destination? ______
3. She immediately questioned the suspect. ______
4. Once upon a time there was a dark secret. ______
5. The school was closed last week. ______
6. He only played twice for his club before he was dropped. ______
7. The girls moved very gracefully in the ballet. ______
8. The team did not play well enough to win the cup. ______

5. Replace the underlined words below with an adverb. Write the new sentences.

1. Dinah looked at the playground <u>in a strange way</u>. ______
2. She answered the questions put by the headmaster <u>in a skilful manner</u>. ______
3. The tallest girl took a pace <u>to the front</u>. ______
4. Lucy chewed at her bottom lip <u>in a miserable way</u>. ______
5. She stepped back and heard them start up <u>one more time</u>. ______
6. <u>In silence</u>, they began to march forward. ______
7. <u>At last</u> Dinah saw what she should do. ______
8. The prefects looked <u>in doubt</u> at each other. ______

6. Fill in the blank spaces using suitable adverbs from the boxes below and write the sentences into your copybook.

away | along | slowly | often | loudly | cruelly | cautiously | quietly

quickly | suddenly | who | very | where | around | that

_______________ Dinah looked out of the window. She saw two of the children walking ______________ across the playground. They looked around ________________ to see _________________ was watching them. They seemed __________________ scared as they whispered ______________ about what had happened _____________ day. The other girls gathered ______________ and started to mock them _________________. They jeered ____________ and laughed as they went _________________ to join their line in the playground. The two children walked _________________ quickly. __________________ were they going? ___________________ Dinah saw the Headmaster walk __________________ after them.

C. Proverbs

Definition box

A proverb is a short clever saying, usually containing a useful or well-known truth or lesson.

1. Write what you think these proverbs mean.

1. Absence makes the heart grow fonder. ______________________
2. Birds of a feather stick together. ______________________
3. When the cat's away the mice will play. ______________________
4. Every cloud has a silver lining. ______________________
5. Make hay while the sun shines. ______________________

2. Compose your own ending for each of the following proverbs.

1. A rolling stone ______________________
2. The early bird ______________________
3. New brooms ______________________
4. One man's meat is ______________________
5. Empty vessels make ______________________

3. Make a class proverb book. Use the proverbs you have collected in your writing.

D. Comedy TV show

Dinah thought that the children in the playground would be telling jokes from the *Eddy Hair Show*. What kind of jokes might she have expected to hear? Tell the class two of your favourite jokes which could be included in a comedy TV show.

E. Capital knowledge

1. Lucy was upset because she did not know her capital cities. Would you get into trouble with the demon headmaster for not knowing your capitals? Check yourself out here!

1. The capital of France is ______________________.
2. The capital of Spain is ______________________.
3. The capital of the USA is ______________________.
4. The capital of Ireland is ______________________.
5. The capital of Japan is ______________________.
6. The capital of Australia is ______________________.
7. The capital of Scotland is ______________________.
8. The capital of Italy is ______________________.
9. The capital of Russia is ______________________.
10. The capital of Argentina is ______________________.

2. Take out your atlas and make up another capitals quiz (or another geography quiz) to give to a partner to complete.

____

____

____

____

____

____

____

____

Don't Be Scared

Writing exercises

1. In her poem, Carol Ann Duffy tries to persuade a child that there is no need to be afraid of the dark. When we are young we are often scared of many things. Think of something else that a young child might be scared of and write five things you might say to the child to calm their fears.

Afraid of ______________________
1.
2.
3.
4.
5.

2. Imagine Carol Ann Duffy asked for your help to write a poem called 'Be Brave' based on the light instead of the dark. What would you write?

Be Brave

By ______________________________

The light is ____________________________________

____

The light is ____________________________________

____

The light is ____________________________________

____

The light is ____________________________________

____

The light is ____________________________________

____

So ____

____

And Be Brave.

Clever challenges

Imagine that you are moving to a new school and that your teacher has to send on a report about you. What do you think your teacher would say about you? Using the following headings, write the report.

Name of Pupil: ______________________

Date of Birth: ______________________

Test scores: Literacy: _______________ Mathematics: __________________

Personality: ____

____

____

Behaviour: ____

____

____

____

Study habits: ____

____

____

Strengths: ____

____

____

General comments: ____

____

____

____

The Hobbit

Word bank

wizard quest encounters morsel blade champ mutters hinges easy chestnut poser mail devours gnaws ogres slays

The Hobbit

1. J.R.R. Tolkien did not draw a picture of a hobbit. Many artists have drawn their own interpretations based on Tolkien's pen picture in his book. Read the excerpt below and draw your own version of a hobbit from this description.

They are (or were) a little people, about half our height, and smaller than the bearded dwarves. Hobbits have no beards…They are inclined to be fat in the stomach; they dress in bright colours (chiefly green and yellow); wear no shoes, because their feet grow natural leathery soles and thick warm brown hair like the stuff on their heads (which is curly); have long clever brown fingers, good-natured faces and laugh deep fruity laughs (especially after dinner, which they have twice a day when they can get it).

2. Think of five riddles that Bilbo Baggins might ask Gollum.

Riddle	Answer
1.	
2.	
3.	
4.	
5.	

3. *The Hobbit* is about a journey from Hobbiton to the Misty Mountains where an evil dragon is guarding a hoard of gold. Brainstorm the dangers the company might face during their adventure, then complete this map, showing and labelling the imaginary and dangerous places the company has to pass through.

4. In this excerpt from *The Hobbit*, the dragon Smaug is attacking the Lake-town of Esgaroth and the townspeople are trying to defend it with bows and arrows. Read it and imagine the scene.

> *...Roaring he swept back over the town...Fire leaped from the dragon's jaws. He circled for a while high in the air above them, lighting all the lake; the trees by the shore shone like copper and like blood with leaping shadows of dense black at their feet. Then down he swooped straight through the arrow-storm, reckless in his rage, taking no heed to turn his scaly sides towards his foes, seeking only to set their town ablaze.*

Using the vivid description above, illustrate the image of the dragon attacking the town.

Tolkien and his world

Word bank

fluently exploring inspiration spectacular reflected acquired depicting lieutenant invalid linguist mythical reclaim invisibility companions epic treachery loyalty comradeship triumphs immortality supreme excavated forged bestowed dimension opposition corrupt influence vampire

A. Comprehension questions

Answer the following questions about the author J.R.R. Tolkien using properly constructed sentences.

1. From where did Tolkien get the name for Bilbo Baggins's home? ______________________________
2. What local landmark might have inspired 'The Two Towers'? ______________ ______________________________
3. What mountains could be the real 'Misty Mountains'? ______________ ______________________________
4. Where did he get the idea for the character of 'Gandalf'? ______________ ______________________________
5. How did most of Tolkien's friends from his youth die? ______________ ______________________________
6. What famous book was the sequel to The Hobbit? ______________ ______________________________
7. Who is Sauron? ______________________________ ______________________________
8. What powers did the One Ring bestow on the wearer? ______________ ______________________________
9. Who were the members of the fellowship? ______________ ______________________________
10. What are 'Sindarin' and 'Quenya'? ______________ ______________________________

B. Word magic

Definition box

A suffix is a group of letters added to the end of a word which changes its meaning.

1. List words that end with these suffixes.

-less powerless	-ness dampness	-ment statement
-ful spoonful	-ish selfish	-ly awfully
-some handsome	-ed gifted	-er miner

2. Choose a word from the box to complete each of the following sentences.

washable	feverish	handful	careless	rectory	heavily	quickly	spoonful

1. The label on my jacket said it was ______________ but when I put it in the machine it was ruined.
2. Dad likes a ______________ of sugar in his tea.
3. It has rained ______________ for a whole week.
4. When I was ill I was very ______________.
5. A clergyman often lives in a house called a ______________.
6. The officer ordered the soldiers to march ______________.
7. I have only a ______________ of marbles left after the game.
8. Susan is very ______________ with her toys and now most of them are broken.

3. Read the story again. List the words you find with prefixes and suffixes.

______________ ______________
______________ ______________
______________ ______________
______________ ______________
______________ ______________

4. Now write four sentences using these words, but leave out the words with prefixes or suffixes and give them to the person beside you to complete.

____
____
____
____
____

Clever challenges

J.R.R. Tolkien was great friends with the author of *The Lion, the Witch and the Wardrobe*. Do you know this book? What's the author's name? Give five similarities and five differences between his and Tolkien's great work of fiction.

The Great Gilly Hopkins

Word bank

bubble gum social worker cautious manoeuvre caseworker flinched professional straggly bangs cripes sincere salvage elaborately satisfaction obligingly towelette guck gruesome penned potbelly hippopotamus blubber freak metal-rimmed mammoth crammed housedress squat slumped lowering bolster repertory barracuda laboriously hefting gross

A. Setting the scene

1. The social worker in the story, Miss Ellis, is obviously being very patient with Gilly. There are certain things that she cannot say in public! Think of some comments she might make about Gilly in private. Finish these starters.

1. You'd really think that ______________________
2. Why can't she ______________________
3. I'm fed up with ______________________
4. I wish that ______________________
5. I hope she's not ______________________
6. She's really ______________________
7. Wouldn't it be ______________________
8. Oh no! Not ______________________

2. We learned that Gilly had a number of foster mothers already. Based on the slight information we were given, write a short piece about each of these characters.

Mrs Nevins	
Mrs Richmond	
Mrs Newman	

B. Gilly's report

In the story it was obvious that Miss Ellis was fed up with Gilly's behaviour. Imagine she has a report about Gilly in her briefcase. Write what you think is in the report. (Under each 'Date' describe when and how she misbehaved.)

Name: ______________________________

Age: ______________________________

Date: ______________________________

____

____

Date: ______________________________

____

____

Date: ______________________________

____

____

My opinion: ______________________________

____

____

____

Signed: ______________________________

Date: ______________________________

C. Character description

1. In this story, the author builds up a picture of Gilly Hopkins through her words. Write your own description of her character using words and phrases from the story as well as words of your own.

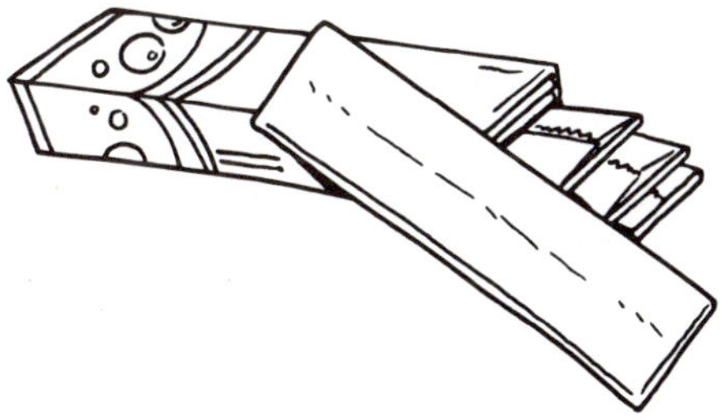

____

____

____

____

____

____

____

____

____

____

2. Think about the different and interesting characters you read about in this story. Make a personal response to them.

I like ________________________ best in this story.

This is because ____

____

____

____

____

I do not like ______________________ in this story.

This is because ____

____

____

____

____

I would like to meet ___________________ from this story.

This is because ____

____

____

____

____

Clever challenges

1. What do you think of Mrs Trotter? Imagine the kind of things she would often say. Draw her portrait and include what you think are her 'catch phrases' in speech bubbles around her.

2. Imagine it is your job to find foster homes for children like Gilly. Write a description of the types of homes and families you require.

3. Write an advertisement, to be published in the local newspaper, looking for foster families.

The Cinnamon Tree

Word bank

grinding slab maize unground grindstone cramping rumbled treble orphan demon snorted blazing taboo betray compound thatched cooped up booby trap lush pattering anxiety squatted gaped landmark illegal tight-rope hoofprint momentarily cinnamon spicy entice agile coiled upward landmine suspended jostling overpowering tremulous flank stickle subsiding unrepentant bride-price

A. Life in Africa

1. Make a list of what you imagine are Yola's daily chores.

2. Read this story again and do some research on Africa.

K What do you know about life in Africa?	W What do you want to know about life in Africa?	L What have you learned about life in Africa?

B. Direct and indirect speech

Definition box

Direct speech means the words actually spoken by a person. Inverted commas are used to show direct speech. Direct speech can be changed to indirect speech.

Example
Gabbin said, 'I don't want the demon to get you.' (direct speech)
Gabbin said that he did not want the demon to get her. (indirect speech)

1. Change these sentences to indirect speech.

1. 'Get him back Yola please,' Gabin begged. ____________________
   ____
2. 'They didn't catch up this time,' said Tom. ____________________
   ____
3. She shouted, 'Stay where you are – I'm coming.' ____________
   ____
4. 'We will be back very soon,' Aki said. 'With your mother.' ____________
   ____
5. 'Which way did he go?' she asked. ____________________
   ____
6. 'It's a time lock, see,' he said, 'so it'll take a couple of minutes.' ________
   ____
7. 'Don't worry,' Yola said, 'I will keep to the paths the grown-ups use every day.'
   ____
   ____
8. He said to himself, 'Well if nobody else will marry Yola, I will.' ________
   ____

2. Change these sentences to direct speech.

1. The teacher sadly told the children she was leaving the school. ____________

   ____

2. The people said that they would help to find the child. ____________

   ____

3. The small boy said that he was frightened of going through the forest in the dark. ____________

   ____

4. We all agreed that the best way forward was to have a meeting about the problem. ____________

   ____

5. He explained that he would climb the mountain first and then swim in the sea.

   ____

   ____

6. The girls said that they would go on an exciting holiday to a place where they had never been. ____________

   ____

7. Alan said he knew the answer to the problem, but he would not share it with the class. ____________

   ____

8. The principal said that the school would close for the holidays on the last day of the month. ____________

   ____

C. Parts of speech

Read the story *The Cinnamon Tree* again and list below the parts of speech that you found in the story.

Nouns	Verbs	Adjectives	Adverbs

Pronouns	Conjunctions	Prepositions

Zlata's diary

A. Personal response

1. Finish one of the following paragraph starters.

- *While reading Zlata's diary excerpts I felt...*
- *While reading the diary I was shocked that...*
- *Zlata's diary made me realise that...*

2. Read Zlata's diary again. Imagine you are her mother. Write some of the entries her mother might have made to describe the same events.

B. Compare and contrast

Zlata's life	Yola's and Gabbin's Life

Clever challenges

1. Imagine you are a reporter for a local newspaper. You are told to interview Zlata about her experiences. Write the questions you would like to put to her.

2. Zlata decides to write about her situation to a relative in a peaceful country asking for help. Write the letter Zlata will send.

3. Zlata has moved to Ireland and is now a pupil in your school. One day she tells her sad story to the class. Retell her story by writing it from the heart.

Lights! Camera! Action!

Word bank

modern production director assemble glittering premiere techniques technology spectacular dramatic stunts impression explosion hinged compressed protection pyrotechnists grenades flammable propane illusion construct gruesome

A. Film favourites

1. List your eight favourite films of all time.

1. ______
2. ______
3. ______
4. ______
5. ______
6. ______
7. ______
8. ______

2. Choose one of the films you have listed and write a summary of the plot.

______

______

______

______

______

______

______

______

3. Who is your favourite film star? Research this person and write a short biography of her/his life in your copybook. Illustrate your biography with cut-out pictures from magazines.

B. Perfect punctuation

In order to be a good writer, you should proofread what you write by rereading it, checking the content, punctuation and grammar.

1. Make a list of the things that you need to look out for when you edit a piece of writing. Draw up a short code for these e.g., C = capitals, Gr = grammar, R = repetition, etc.

____

____

____

____

____

____

____

____

2. Rewrite this passage from *The Lion, the Witch and the Wardrobe* putting in the correct punctuation and capital letters. Compare it to a partner's when finished.

> *this must be a simply enormous wardrobe thought lucy going further in and pushing the soft folds of the coats aside to make room for her feet I wonder is that more moth-balls she thought stooping down to feel it with her hand but instead of feeling the hard smooth wood of the floor of the wardrobe she felt something soft and powdery and extremely cold this is very queer she said and went on a step or two further*

C. Story boards and stunts

1. Imagine you are a film director. Choose one of the stories in your Anthology that you would like to make into a film. Create a storyboard in pictures to represent the scenes you will portray in your film.

2. Choose a stunt that you will have to stage for your film. Think about how you will do it and what technology you might need to help you. Describe what you will do.

____

____

____

____

____

____

____

____

____

____

D. Synonyms

Definition box

Synonyms are words or phrases that mean exactly or nearly the same as another word or phrase.

1. Rewrite this passage in your copybook, putting in suitable synonyms for the underlined words. Use a thesaurus to help you.

He had to slow down for Derval. She was running as fast as she could. The lane twisted a lot, and then they came to a place where it was bisected by a slow-moving river. The river looked clean and ran over gravel. He bent down. 'On my back!' he said to her. She put her arms around his neck, and he ran straight into the river.

2. Brainstorm synonyms for these words and make your own word webs.

sad

big

walk

said

nice

ate

cruel

small

bad

good

3. Create a class word bank of your synonyms.

The Thornthwaite Inheritance

Word bank

inheritance truce attempted cunning revolution aristocrat guillotine triggered squabble illegal bottle-green self-defence self-preservation motivation propose quits piranha booby-trapped device spire suspiciously tactic unleashing lethal sincerity ceasefire ensuring tampered untimely demise circumstances sumptuous conclusion plausible post-mortem bloodstream caviar draped decanter ominously reflect profound mantelshelf earpiece foundations overdeveloped forensic conclusive

A. Plotting murder

1. Imagine two other murder plots that these children could have hatched. Describe what you think they might have planned.

Lorelli's plot	Ovid's plot

2. Think about the story you have just read and complete these paragraphs.

My personal opinion of the story is ______________________________

____

____

____

____

____

This is because ____

____

____

____

____

____

What in this story reminds you of something in real life? ____

____

____

____

____

____

3. In this story the author leaves us wondering about what happens next. What do you think happens? Write the next part of the story.

____

____

____

____

____

____

____

____

B. Homonyms

Definition box

Homonyms are words that sound the same but have different meanings.

1. Write a homonym for each word in the list.

great		made	
seller		blew	
flower		feet	
pair		leak	
steak		son	
hole		wait	
key		scene	
boy		sew	
right		hair	
wood		none	

2. Redraft the following sentences, correcting the homonyms.

1. Their had to be a mist or Jessie wood knot even try it.
2. She wanted know one else too know about it.
3. Know one must sea her.
4. If she was going two fail again she wood fail alone.
5. Jessie new what was waiting for her.
6. It was balance that was the reel problem.
7. Her hare shone in the son.

3. Write a short paragraph using incorrect homonyms in your copybook and swap it with the person beside you. Redraft their paragraph, correcting the homonyms.

C. Responding to characters

Ovid suggested that they call a truce. 'I no longer want to kill you,' he announced, his bottle-green eyes meeting his sister's across the table.

1. When you read this piece about Ovid how did it make you feel?

2. What words would you use to describe the character of Ovid?

3. Look at the story again. What else do you learn about Ovid's character and his family set-up?

4. How do you think Detective Skinner felt about the Thornthwaite family?

5. What is your opinion of this family? Use evidence from the text to support your answer.

____

____

____

____

____

____

____

____

D. Be a television producer

Imagine you are a television producer. You can choose and produce your own programmes. What programme would you like to make? Fill in the information about it on this and the next page.

Name of programme: ____________________________________

Director: ____________________________________

Scriptwriter: ____________________________________

Camera: ____________________________________

Lighting: ____________________________________

Sound: ____________________________________

Camera instructions	Script
1. Focus at a distance 2. 3. 4.	
1. 2. 3. 4.	
1. 2. 3. 4. Slow fade out	

Clever challenges

1. 'Cats have nine lives' is a well-known saying. Invent a cat character and draw a cartoon strip to show how your cat really needed his nine lives. Make it as funny as possible!

2. DI Lionel Skinner is a detective. Think of other famous detective characters from novels, films or TV. Write a short piece about one of these characters.

Three Irish poets

Word bank

myths mysticism fascination mythology reputation recognition enwrought tread scholarship mysterious soldering gleaming fluent imagination competition editor emboldened enthusiasm

A. Poets and their poems

1. It is often said, 'The poet is the poem's first critic.'
Do you think this is true of any artist? Is the artist, for example, the first critic of his/her painting? Is the musician the first critic of his/her album? Are you your own first critic? Write a short piece about this idea.

____

____

____

____

____

____

____

____

2. Complete the following sentence for each of the three poems featured in the Anthology.

My favourite line in 'Aedh Wishes for the Cloth of Heaven' is '________________

____'.

This is because ____.

My favourite line in 'When All the Others' is '________________________'.

This is because ____.

My favourite line in 'Bully' is '________________________________'.

This is because ____.

3. Seamus Heaney said that poetry is always slightly mysterious, and he wondered what his relationship was to it. What is your relationship to poetry? Write about it here.

____

____

____

____

____

____

____

____

____

4. Write three acrostic poems based on key words from these poems.

B ________	**H** ________	**P** ________
U ________	**E** ________	**O** ________
L ________	**A** ________	**T** ________
L ________	**V** ________	**A** ________
Y ________	**E** ________	**T** ________
	N ________	**O** ________
		E ________
		S ________

5. Use your research tools to find out more about your favourite poet.

6. Write a brief information piece about each of the three poets in your copybook.

B. Word work – prefixes and suffixes

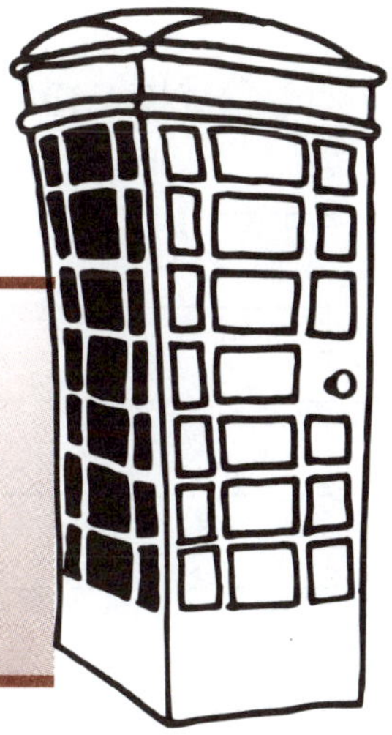

Definition box

Prefixes come *before* words.
Suffixes come *after* words.
Sometimes you can add both a prefix and a suffix to a word.

Example
Replacement   importer

1. Make new words by adding a prefix, a suffix or both to the words below.

rag	care	act
place	phone	press
mill	port	vent

2. Now put five of your new words into sentences to show their meanings.

____

____

____

____

____

C. Revising parts of speech

Read the following extract from a novel called *Thunder and Lightnings* and list the parts of speech in the categories below.

Andrew was not surprised. Victor's writing was a sort of code to deceive the enemy, with punctuation marks in unlikely places to confuse anyone who came too close to cracking the code. He watched Andrew counting the full stops in one sentence and said, 'I put those in while I think about the next word. I like doing question marks better.' He pointed out two or three specimens, independent question marks, without questions.
They looked like curled feathers out of a pillow. One had a face.

Nouns	Verbs	Adjectives	Adverbs

Pronouns	Conjunctions	Prepositions

Clever challenges

Creating images in our minds helps us understand poetry as we read it.
Read the three poems again. Choose one to discuss through your senses.

What do you see?

What are the smells around you?

What sounds do you hear?

What can you taste as you read?

What can you touch?

Searching the small ads

Word bank

hobbies electronics reduced features digital warrior badminton racquet experienced intermediate official hilarious antique prestigious processor condition graphics realistic restrung punctual

A. Important information

1. Advertisements must be short and to the point. List the most important information to be included in an advertisement.

_______________ _______________ _______________ _______________

_______________ _______________ _______________ _______________

2. Write out a small ad for three of these items in the boxes below.

- Your cat has had kittens and you need good homes for them.
- You have an old broken-down piano for sale.
- You have just opened a shop that sells second-hand clothes.
- You are an artist with paintings of local scenes for sale.
- You have a large garden and you want to rent part of it out as allotments.
- You have a mobile home beside the sea to rent for family holidays.
- You are a witch with magic potions for sale.
- You are Prince Charming searching for Cinderella.
- You want to start a new pop group.

3. The following storybook characters need to place an advertisement. In your copybook, write the ads you think they posted.

- Santa Claus wants a new assistant.
- The Demon Headmaster needs new teachers.
- The Thornthwaites need a new butler.
- Gilly Hopkins needs new foster parents.
- Bilbo Baggins needs a travel companion.

B. Antonyms

Definition box

An antonym is a word that has the opposite meaning of another word.

1. Find the antonyms of the words below.

possible	safe	heavy	adult	transparent
______	______	______	______	______
exit	exhale	increase	simple	happy
______	______	______	______	______
polite	talkative	agree	handsome	selfish
______	______	______	______	______
	thaw	plenty	colourful	
	______	______	______	

2. Choose six of the word pairs and put each pair into a sentence.

3. In your copybook, create an antonym quiz for a friend.

C. Homonyms

Definition box

Remember: Some homonyms are spelt and pronounced in the same way but have different meanings.

Example ruler
I used my ruler to measure my desk.
The White Witch was the ruler of Narnia.

1. Choose eight words from this list and write sentences to show their meanings.

grave	blade	flag
date	graze	nail
box	game	bat
bill	scale	corn
draw	court	hail
crow	crane	club
palm	sound	comb
set	perch	spring

2. Think of other homonyms like these and make a list. Compare your list to your partner's beside you.

____

____

____

____

____

3. Write sentences to show the meanings of five of the homonyms in the list you have compiled.

____

____

____

____

____

D. Code breakers

Codes can be created in a variety of ways.

1. Create a code by assigning a number to each letter of the alphabet. Write some coded messages and give them to the person beside you to solve.

a	b	c	d	e	f	g	h	i	j	k	l	m
n	o	p	q	r	s	t	u	v	w	x	y	z

2. Encode a sentence by breaking it into groups of letters and swap your coded sentence with the person beside you.

Example
I like to read and write at school
IL IK ET OR EA DA ND WR IT EA TS CH OO L

3. Create a code by assigning a symbol to each letter of the alphabet. Write some messages using this code and give them to the person beside you to solve.

a	b	c	d	e	f	g	h	i	j	k	l	m
n	o	p	q	r	s	t	u	v	w	x	y	z

Clever challenges

1. In drama-script form, write the phone conversation between yourself and one of the advertisers featured in your Anthology (you believe that the advertiser has something to hide!).

2. Some ads are written especially for radio. This involves a different way of getting the message across. Write the wording for radio ads for two of the following products. Form a group with some friends, select a piece of music to introduce the ad or as a background for it, and perform it for the class.

- Waifos Watery Biscuits
- Confreys Coconut Shampoo
- Monica's Magic Moisturiser
- Lovely Long Lined Gloves
- Crispy Cabbage and Carrot Soup

Inkheart

Word bank

mysteriously bookbinder fencing torture revenge miracle sea-serpent ancient pirate hobgoblin suspense sinister central heating marten bookmark outright clutched stammered paralysed wide-eyed entangled accursed talkative reassuring fatal wretched brandishing reeling flinched cowered scampered silken drunkenly midge transparent

A. Favourite childhood books

1. Do you remember your favourite picture books and storybooks that you read when you were younger? List some of the book titles here.

____

____

____

____

____

2. Choose one of the books or stories and explain why this story or book is special to you and retell the story below.

____

____

____

____

____

____

____

____

____

____

____

3. Design a book jacket for one of your favourite books.

B. Types of books

In this story Mo is an expert bookbinder. He buys crates full of books, lots of different types of books. Name as many different types of books as you can think of.

C. Imagine this!

1. If you could conjure up a storybook character by reading about him/her out loud, which character/characters would you choose? Why?

____

____

____

____

____

2. In this story the author leaves us wondering about Meggie's mother. What do you think happened to her? Write your explanation.

____

____

____

____

____

____

____

____

Clever challenges

1. Meggie's mother loved a book 'to lead her into an unknown land'. What book took you into an unknown land far away from your everyday life? Describe that place.
2. In this story we are told that *fear tastes quite different when you are not just reading about it*. In your opinion what does that taste like? Describe the taste.
3. When a description is vivid, it helps us to form clear visual images in our mind's eye. The author of this story creates vivid images for us through the use of language. Choose your favourite image and draw it.
4. Complete one of the following paragraph starters.
   - *I think Mo showed a lot of bravery in this story when...*
   - *I can tell that Meggie's mother was a great reader because...*
   - *The characters who emerged from the book were...*

Get there on time

Word bank

passengers operates general abbreviations symbols standard accommodation buffet connecting schedules advance stations

A. Timetables

1. Draw up a school timetable

	Monday	Tuesday	Wednesday	Thursday	Friday
9.00 – 10.00					
10.00 – 11.00					

2. Find another type of timetable and stick it into your copybook. Then write down ten pieces of factual information you learned from examining it.

3. Invent a timetable for a *favourite character* from literature.

	Mon	Tue	Wed	Thur	Fri
Morning					
Afternoon					
Evening					
Night					

B. Mapping

1. Draw a map of Ireland. Plot the journey from Dublin to Ennis by train on the map. Using a different colour, plot the journey by bus.

2. Which mode of transport would you prefer and why?

C. Compare and contrast

1. Compare the advantages and disadvantages of both forms of transport.

Travel by train

Advantages	Disadvantages

Travel by bus

Advantages	Disadvantages

2. Conduct a class survey to find out which type of transport is more popular.

D. Perfect punctuation

Rewrite this passage from a story called *The Exiles* by Hilary McKay, adding the correct punctuation. Swap with a partner to correct your work.

Hes just not replied Phoebe anyway Im fed up of this Im going to bury him now the career of a racing maggot inevitably ended in burial it hid the evidence what happened to the maggots afterwards was a mystery although Rachel and Phoebe had often tried digging them up again to find out perhaps they crawled away or a bird ate them either would be better than their original fate on the end of a hook

E. Apostrophes – possession

Definition box

We use an apostrophe to show that something belongs to someone.

1. Ask your friends about their favourite things. List them below.

Friend	Favourite Things
Jane	ice hockey

2. Now write sentences using the information above. Don't forget to include the apostrophe!

Example
Jane's favourite sport is ice hockey.

____

____

____

____

____

____

____

Definition box

To show that something belongs to more than one person add an apostrophe after the -s.

Example
The girls' hats

If the plural is formed without an -s, you put the apostrophe at the end of the word and add the -s after it.

Example
The children's coats

3. Rewrite these sentences adding apostrophes.

1. Michaels eyes were calm and kind, he thought. ______________________

    ____

2. Harper set down the flask before returning the childs embrace. ______________________

    ____

3. Morning, noon and evening the muezzins call to prayer used to echo out across the city. ______________________

    ____

4. At that moment the silence of the valley was shattered by the bells of Glendaloughs seven churches. ______________________

    ____

5. The farmhouse had been Grans before she'd deeded it over to Elizabeths father and his family the year she'd moved north. ______________________

    ____

6. The workmens bell was fixed in this tree. ______________________

    ____

F. Apostrophes – contractions

Definition box

An apostrophe is also used to show where letters have been left out.

1. Rewrite the following using apostrophes.

you will	______	could not	______
let us	______	do not	______
I am	______	are not	______
we are	______	that is	______
I have	______		

Its and it's are often confused.
It's is short for it is or it has. The apostrophe replaces the missing letter.
Its is used to show possession.

Example
It's raining cats and dogs.
The dog ate its dinner.

2. Rewrite the following sentences using *its* or *it's*.

1. 'Finn! Finn! ________our own Uncle Toby.'
2. The evening ran ________usual course.
3. '________ so dark – do you think we have far to go?'
4. '________absolutely fabulous, Mum,' she breathed.
5. The snow appeared to fall from ________ upper storeys.

The Eyeball Collector

Word bank

cursed rotated stench menacing ominous unrelenting cobbled converged regardless ventured vagabond light-fingered claustrophobic pickpocket sharp-eyed encircling queried feeble unimpressed sarcasm artfully albeit half-heartedly outnumbered hostile inwardly appease captor snigger unnervingly surged onslaught assailant cravat inadvertently cocoon inevitable brazenly guffawing ruefully sophistication exasperation cajoled

A. For and against

1. In Hector's story certain crimes were punishable by death. In some parts of the world capital punishment is still used. What is your opinion about this? Write down your ideas.

For capital punishment	Against capital punishment

2. Now have a class debate on the topic. Which argument wins?

B. Creating suspense

Chapter one: Southbound
Tartri flammis! cursed Hector as his stomach tightened in a knot and his chest jerked violently with every beat of his heart. He rotated slowly on the spot, panting from the chase. His nose tingled with the stench that filled the air.

Using the above chapter starter, write an alternative story to the one in your Anthology.

C. Powerful adjectives

Definition box

An adjective is a word or a short phrase used to describe a noun.
There are different types of adjectives as we have already seen.

1. When an author chooses an adjective to describe a noun, it sometimes needs to be a more powerful or intense word to grip the reader and create more suspense.

Put the adjectives in each line in order from the weakest to the most powerful.

1. sad	miserable	upset	wretched
2. freezing	chilly	cold	cool
3. big	enormous	gigantic	huge
4. starving	hungry	peckish	ravenous
5. ecstatic	happy	delighted	pleased
6. tired	drowsy	sleepy	exhausted
7. hot	boiling	lukewarm	warm

2. Fill in the missing adjectives from the ordinary to the most intense.

pleased			ecstatic
able			genius
irritated			furious
worried			petrified
upset			wretched
big			gigantic
lukewarm			boiling
drowsy			exhausted

D. Powerful feelings

In *The Eyeball Collector*, F.E. Higgins describes the feeling of fear at the beginning of the story. Read the first paragraph again and note the last line: *So this is fear, he thought. In a strange way it excited him.*

1. Use your senses and your text to help you think of 'fear' words and phrases.

What does fear look like?	What does fear sound like?	What does fear smell like?	What does fear feel like?	What does fear taste like?

2. Compose a senses poem based on FEAR in the framework below.
   - use your word and phrase bank above to help you
   - put your lines in any order you like
   - write several drafts if you wish
   - do not forget to proofread and edit it to improve it
   - write your final draft
   - illustrate your poem.

Fear

Fear is a ______________________________

It looks like ______________________________

It smells like ______________________________

It feels like ______________________________

It tastes like ______________________________

It sounds like ______________________________

Fear is ______________________________

Make a class book of 'Fear Poetry'.

Two poems

Read the two poems 'A Fortunate Find' and 'Where Is It?'
Discuss them.

How are they alike?

____

____

____

How are they different?

____

____

____

Did you like the poems? Which did you prefer?

____

____

____

How did these poems make you feel?

____

____

____

Clever challenges

1. If you could have intervened and stopped the action at any time in this story, where would it have been? What would you have done? Write about it.

2. Describe how you managed to escape from a difficult or dangerous situation. Use the following starter sentence.

   'Now I'm for it,' I thought...

3. Hector has returned home and is describing life on the other side. Write his account of it.

4. Find five more word puzzles to share with your class.

No Passengers Beyond This Point

Word bank

faucet evidence crabby cafeteria iffy clearinghouse bunker recycling magnet permission slip resemble league eraser assignment skittering hyperventilate irritated zits overstuffed speciality automatically hick semester accredited register beanbag cowering quarantine concede

A. Personal writing

Finn and his sisters obviously feel that their world is being 'turned upside down'. Write a short piece about a time when you felt like this.

B. Interview

Imagine you are an author and are being interviewed. Here are the interviewer's questions.

1. What are the topics you most like to write about?
2. Do you prefer to write fiction or non-fiction?
3. Do you find it easy to write?
4. Where is your favourite place for writing?
5. From where do you get your writing ideas?
6. Are you inspired by any other authors in your writing?
7. Do you illustrate your own writing?
8. What advice would you give to other writers?

Think about the questions, make short notes about the answers you will give, and then write out the answers in your copybook.

C. More about idioms

1. In this story the children's *world is turned upside down*. The world is not physically or actually turning upside down, rather it is an idiomatic way of saying that everything is upset or changed in a worrying way. Write the meaning of the following idioms.

Idiom	I think it means...
■ went pear shaped	
■ the apple of my eye	
■ bend over backwards	
■ scrape the bottom of the barrel	
■ full of beans	
■ spill the beans	
■ rings a bell	
■ rock the boat	
■ carry the can	

2. Write a sentence for each one in your copybook to show you understand the meaning.

3. Rewrite the following sentences replacing the idioms with ordinary speech.

1. Don't beat about the bush, tell us what happened. ______________________

____

2. I was over the moon with the good news. ______________________________

____

3. He was taken for a ride when he made that purchase. __________________

____

4. I feel under the weather today so I'll stay in bed. ____________________

____

5. If you scratch my back I'll scratch yours. ______________________________

____

6. It was so over the top, I refused to wear it.______________________________

____

7. I do not agree with it but it is par for the course. ____________________

____

D. Complex sentences

Definition box

A simple sentence has only one clause/sentence and cannot be broken up into smaller sentences.

Example
My sisters don't worry at all.

A complex sentence has more than one clause joined by link words or conjunctions.

Each clause can stand on its own.

Example
I'm out there every morning doing drills, and I go to practice every afternoon.

Definition box

A complex sentence has a main clause and one or more subordinate clauses. A subordinate clause cannot stand on its own. It depends on the main clause to make sense.

Example

India rolls her eyes when she talks to me about this.

'India rolls her eyes' is the main clause.

'When she talks to me about this' is a subordinate clause. It depends on the main clause to make sense.

Find the main clause and the subordinate clause/clauses in these sentences. (Underline the verbs – this will help you identify the clauses.)

1. Roald Dahl wrote many books which enchanted every child the world over.

Main clause: ____________________

Subordinate clause: ____________________

____

2. Black Beauty took five years to write because Anna Sewell was very ill.

Main clause: ____________________

Subordinate clause: ____________________

____

3. After we had supper, everyone helped to clear the table.

Main clause: ____________________

Subordinate clause: ____________________

____

4. It was clear that he had been badly injured when his car hit the ditch.

Main clause: ____________________

Subordinate clause: ____________________

____

5. It was a wild winter's evening when Mr Crutcher answered the door to DI Skinner.

Main clause: ______________________________

Subordinate clause: ______________________________

____

6. Only the foolish followed the narrow paths that led over the hill because the soldiers left their bombs and booby traps all over it.

Main clause: ______________________________

Subordinate clause: ______________________________

____

Clever challenges

1. In this story we read that 'worry is like a leaky faucet – every drip makes you imagine something bad on the way'. Write about a worry you had that turned out well in the end.

2. The characters in this story are very interesting. Choose four characters to write about. What do you learn about them from reading the excerpt? Add your own ideas about them.

3. This story explores the attachment everyone has to their homes. Write about this from your point of view.

4. What do you think homelessness involves? Write about it. Do some research using your research tools.

Debate the issue

Word bank

arguments issue debate discuss opposing supporters control persistent poultry pheasants partridge grouse trapping snaring eventual employment farriers saddlers limestone company rural accessible recreation cultural sentimentality naturalist villain efficient indiscriminate predator scavengers

Summary points

1. In 'Debate the issue' points are made on both sides of the argument 'for' and 'against' fox hunting. Summarise the points in short form using bullet points instead of full sentences.

In support of fox hunting	Against fox hunting

2. What do *you* think? Have a class debate and vote on which side presented the stronger argument.

What it says in the papers

Parts of speech

Look at the two newspaper articles and list the parts of speech under the headings below. Choose your own headings for the final three sections.

Nouns	Adjectives	Adverbs	Pronouns

Prepositions			

The Word Party

Think of your own words or phrases to replace the images in the poem 'The Word Party'. List them below. The first one is suggested for you.

Loving words <u>bring summer posies</u>

Rude words ______________________________

Sly words ______________________________

Short words ______________________________

Common words ______________________________

Complicated words ______________________________

Swear words ______________________________

Hard words ______________________________

Foreign words ______________________________

Careless words ______________________________

Long words ______________________________

Code words ______________________________

Silly words ______________________________

Hyphenated words ______________________________

Strong words ______________________________

Sweet words ______________________________

Kind words ______________________________

Clever challenges

1. Find some interesting headlines in a national or local paper. Paste them into your copybook.
2. Sometimes a headline has very little to do with the story under it, and is designed only to draw your attention to it. Choose one such headline and write an alternative story to go with it.
3. Choose a school event past or present and write an article about it for the school newsletter.

19 Railway Street

Word bank

orphaned privilege impoverished tenement moonlit flannel cambric chambermaid dwindled mademoiselle governess polished speculative writhing sinister suffocated draperies nursery inspiration secreted wardrobe cabinet chamber pot intently stalking staircase cloakroom baize wick aloft carbolic warped materialised battered protruding omen motto veiling frantically snob toff banshee starveling fragment discarded ha'penny translucent defiantly retorted

A. A window on the past

1. Write down some jottings in the diaries of Sophie and Mickser to give a flavour of what a day in the life of each character was like.

Sophie's diary	Mickser's diary
Woke at 8.00, had breakfast of...	

2. Fill in the missing words in these sentences which are all taken from the text of *19 Railway Street*. Check the answers *afterwards* in your book to see how many you had right. Award yourself one point if you had the exact word or half a point if you used a synonym.

1. Sophie Rutledge lives a life of ____________ in a fine Georgian house.
2. Never turn loose of anything valuable, that was his ___________.
3. In spite of the _________ dressing-gown she wore over her __________ nightdress, Sophie shuddered.
4. She was almost, but not quite, ________________.
5. The shadows in the corners were ___________ into sinister shapes.
6. Everyone knew the ________________ were haunted.
7. _______________ did not believe young ladies should have imagination.
8. She wrapped her dressing-gown more ________ round herself and went to the door.
9. He was afraid of _________ bruises, those terrible _________ that came up on bare feet.
10. In a cloakroom off the entrance hall was a green __________ door.

B. Researching and writing

Mickser felt his jaw drop. He did the sums quickly. 'That would make it 1776.' He saw the girl nod. 'But this is 1907!'

1. Read the story again and find evidence in the story about life in 1776.
2. Now find evidence about life in 1907.
3. Research life in the late eighteenth and early twentieth centuries. Share your information with the class.
4. Using all the information you have collected, write a short comparison of Sophie's and Mickser's lives in your copybook.
5. Which of the characters' lives would you prefer, and why?

C. Character mapping

Read the story again and create word maps for Sophie and Mickser.

D. Parts of speech

Read the following extract from *19 Railway Street* and list the parts of speech in the grid below.

The boy gave a cry of surprise and jumped back, but he did not turn loose of the metal bar. Never turn loose of anything valuable, that was his motto. Cobwebs plastered his face, veiling his eyes, clinging to his lips. Frantically he scraped them off...
And met the eyes of a red-haired girl not much older than himself. She was holding onto the other end of the metal bar, which he now recognised as a large, long-tined fork.

Nouns	Verbs	Adjectives	Adverbs

Pronouns	Conjunctions	Prepositions

E. Open the doors

At the bottom of the steps was a row of unpainted timber doors. Each bore a small, neatly lettered sign...

1. Look at each of these doors. List what you think are the contents of each room.

2. Imagine you opened one of these doors. Write about what happened. Don't forget to plan your story first. Make a class book of your stories.

Number 29 Fitzwilliam street

Answer the following questions about Number 29.

1. What does the word 'Georgian' mean? ______________________
2. Who was the first owner of Number 29? ______________________
3. What feature distinguishes Georgian front doors? ______________________
4. Who generally lived on the third floor of a Georgian house? ______________________
5. Why would the top floor be livelier than the rest of the house? ______________________
6. Which part of the house was generally the busiest and why? ______________________
7. What is 'poor man's silver'? ______________________
8. Describe the Housekeeper's job. ______________________
9. What was a 'rat shelf'? ______________________
10. What single item changed people's eating habits in the 1870s? ______________________

Clever challenges

1. Which of the two characters from *19 Railway Street*, Sophie or Mickser, would you like to meet? What would you like to ask them? List your questions.
2. Using your research tools, prepare a fact file of the two historical times in this story.
3. Research Irish folklore and do a mini-project on the Banshee.

River Boy

Word bank

figment down-side hard-core leisurely lemming frustration doggedly telepathy exhalation vulnerable deprived perverse sensation glistening isolation apprehensive contrariness prickly treading consternation hearse exasperated consultant yearning insistence outcome shrift prominent clogged bloody-mindedness loggerheads unambitious exception remote undertaker chuckled vigour reassuring unsettling pondered rendered caustic hovering amorphous eerily resonance ignoramus muse wilful motivate obsessive overwhelmed irresistibly

A. What do you think?

Choose four of the questions below and write the answers in your copybook.

1. Does one of your favourite activities have a downside?
2. What are lemmings famous for?
3. Would you like to be able to communicate through telepathy? Why?
4. Do you ever feel deprived? Give an example.
5. Name some creatures whose life cycles involve a cocoon stage.
6. Do you think you have a good concentration span? Justify your answer.
7. Do you ever feel apprehensive about anything? Give some examples.
8. Does anyone in your family suffer from contrariness? Describe him or her.
9. Are you ever exasperated at things? Explain.
10. Has anyone ever given you 'short shrift'? Who did and why?

B. A seasoned traveller

Pack a suitcase for each of the following trips.

Sun holiday	Skiing holiday	Adventure holiday

C. Be a director

River Boy is being made into a drama. Imagine you are the director. To prepare for this drama you are studying one of the characters from the story. Choose your character and then complete the storyboard below.

First impression: ______________________________

____

____

Appearance: ______________________________

____

____

Words to describe: ______________________________

____

____

Behaviour: ______________________________

____

____

Possible costume design: ______________________________

____

____

How he/she moves: ______________________________

____

____

Type of voice: ______________________________

____

____

Special features: ______________________________

____

____

Final impression: ______________________________

____

____

Two poems

Growing old

1. Compare the two poems 'Lion King' and 'On Aging'. What do they have in common? What is different?

2. Which do you prefer? Why?

3. Consider aging from your own viewpoint and answer the questions below.

1. Are you looking forward to getting older? What do you think your routine will be every day? ______

2. When you are very old, like the character in the poem 'On Aging', what activities might be difficult to do? ______________________________

____

____

____

____

____

____

____

3. What are the advantages to growing old in your opinion? ______________

____

____

____

____

____

____

____

4. Interview a grandparent or older person you know about their experiences of growing old and write up the questions and answers in your copybook.

Clever challenges

1. Who would you describe as being bloody-minded and why?
2. Were you ever at loggerheads with your parents? Give an example.
3. Would you describe yourself as ambitious or unambitious? Why?
4. Describe a DIY project you have undertaken.
5. Have you ever done something on impulse? What did you do?
6. What is the most remote place you have ever visited? Describe it.
7. What puts a sparkle in your eye?
8. What does giving a *caustic response* to someone mean? Have you ever done that? Why?
9. Do you think you are a vain person? Explain.
10. Have you ever been obsessive about something? What and why?
11. Brainstorm what makes you want to buy a book in a bookshop.
12. Imagine you are promoting *River Boy* by Tim Bowler. Read the story again and write a blurb which you will use to promote the book in your local bookshop.
13. Research the author of the book and write a short biographical note about him.
14. Now design your version of the book cover. Don't forget to include:
    - title
    - author
    - publisher
    - ISBN
    - blurb
    - reviews.
15. Design a poster to promote the book.
16. Write a short piece explaining why you think some modern artists do not give names to their pieces of art and often label them *Untitled*.

Poems

Word bank

wily hero destined marvellous scientist musician beautician glade ambition

A. Personal writing

1. Write a short piece on one of the following topics:
   - Life is what you make of it.
   - All men are created equal.
   - You can be anything you want to be.
   - The old have dreams, the young have visions.

   Share your writing with the class.

2. Write a critique of the poem 'From Ithaka'. First, check your dictionary for the meaning of the word critique.

3. Read the poem and think about the ideas in 'You Can't Be That!' What would you like to do in life that your parents might be unhappy about? Explain.

B. Poetry review

Look back at all the poems in your Anthology and complete the following poetry review.

My favourite poem: ____________________

Poet: ____________________

I liked this poem because…

____

____

____

____

Words I liked in this poem:

____

____

____

____

It made me feel…

____

____

____

____

What I would like to say to the poet:

____

____

____

____

Signed: ____________________ Date: ____________________